Alberto
GIACOMETTI

The dream, the Sphinx, and the death of T.

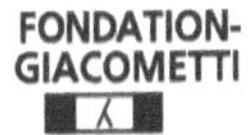

FONDATION-
GIACOMETTI

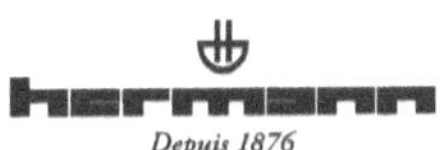

Depuis 1876

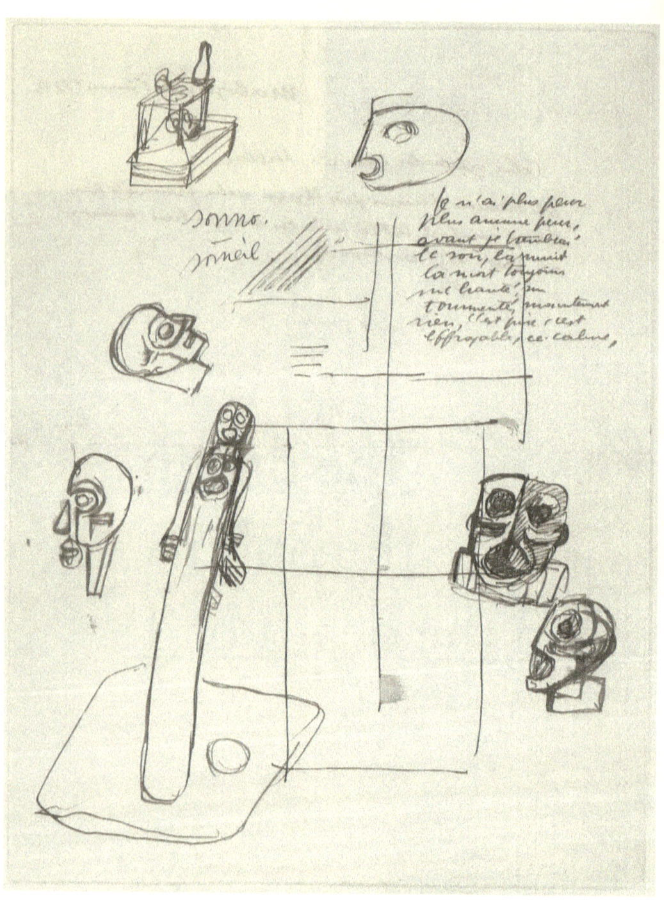

Studies of sculptures and annotations, c. August 1933
Black ink on writing paper, 27 x 21 cm
Fondation Giacometti

I'm no longer frightened
no more fright,
before I used to tremble
evening, night
death always
haunted me,
tormented me, now
nothing, it's worse it's
terrifying, this calm

Around August 1933

<u>The dream,
the Sphinx,
and the death of T.</u>

Frightened, I caught sight of an enormous brown and hairy spider at the foot of my bed whose thread, to which it was attached, connected to a web stretched just above the bolster. 'No, no!' I cried, 'I can't bear spending the night with a threat like that above my head, kill it, kill it!' and I said that with all the disgust I felt at the idea of doing it myself, whether in the dream or in a waking state.

I awoke at that very moment, but I was waking up in the dream that continued. I found myself on the same spot at the foot of the bed and at the precise moment I was saying to myself: 'It was just a dream', I caught sight, while instinctively looking for it, I caught sight of, as if stretched on a pile of earth and fragments of plates or small flat stones, what was a yellow, ivory-yellow spider, much more monstrous than the first, but smooth and seemingly covered in smooth yellow scales, with long and slender legs, that seemed smooth and hard as bones. Terrorised, I saw the hand of my girlfriend move closer and touch the spider's scales; she seemed not to be afraid or surprised. I cried out and pulled her hand away and, as in the dream, I asked for the creature to be killed. Someone I had not seen until that moment squashed it with a long stick or spade, hit it violently and repeatedly and, with my gaze averted, I heard the scales split and the strange noise of the soft parts being crushed. Only after, while looking at the spider's remains spread out on a plate, did I read a name written very clearly in ink on one of the scales. It was the name of a species of Arachnids, a name I can no longer pronounce,

a name I forgot, I can only see the letters standing
out, the black ink on the ivory-yellow, like letters seen
in museums on stones and shells. Evidently, I had
just had a rare specimen belonging to the collection
of the friends I was staying with at the time killed.
That was confirmed a moment later by the grumbling
old governess who came in looking for the lost
spider. My first thought was to tell her what had
just happened, but I could see the disadvantages, the
anger my hosts would feel towards me: I should have
realised it was a rare creature by reading its name
and warned them instead of killing it, so I decided to
say nothing, to pretend I knew nothing and to hide
its remains. I went out into the park with the plate,
I walked through it, taking precautions not to be seen,
the plate in my hands might seem odd, I reached a bit
of land that had been dug, hidden in the undergrowth
at the foot of a slope, and, sure that I had not been
seen, I threw the remains into a hole which I trampled
down, thinking: 'The scales will rot before they are
discovered.' At that same moment, I saw my host and
his daughter riding past on horses on the slope above
me; without stopping, they said a few words to me
that surprised me and I awoke.

For the whole of the next day, I had that spider in
front of my eyes, I was obsessed with it.

The day before, late in the night, I had noticed the
ivory-yellow traces of pus on a glossy white sheet of
paper, and knew that I had caught the illness I had
been expecting for a few days. As I was observing this,

I was thrown by an apparent involuntary paralysis
of the mind that prevented me from cutting short
the threat of the illness, which would have been very
easy to do but which I neglected. Nothing led me
to believe in some kind of self-punishment; I felt
obscurely that the illness could be somehow useful to
me, could bring me advantages whose nature I was not
aware of.

Laying down that night, and a little before the dream,
my friend, while laughing, wanted to assess the
symptoms of my illness.

I had been expecting that illness since the previous
Saturday when, at 6 p.m., hearing that they were going
to close down The Sphinx for ever, I rushed there,
finding it unbearable to think that I would never again
see that room in which I had spent, since its opening,
so many hours, so many evenings, and which for me
was the most splendid of all places.

I went there for the last time a little drunk, after
having lunched with friends. At that lunch we had
talked, in passing, about how interesting it would be
to keep a daily diary and about everything that could
thwart the idea. My immediate desire, which caught
me by surprise, was to start that diary straightaway,
and start at the very moment we were gathered, and
on that subject, Skira asked me to write, for this issue
of *Labyrinthe*, about the story of the death of T. that
I had told him some time before. I promised I would
without thinking clearly of the possibility of doing so.

But since the dream, since the illness that brought me
back to that lunch, the death of T. has become present
in my mind again.

That afternoon, coming back from the doctor,
I wondered if the timely coincidence of that request
from Skira and the visit to The Sphinx with what
followed was enough to impose on me the memory
of the death of T., to give me today the desire to write
about it. I must mention here that as I was coming
out of the pharmacy, the tubes of Thiazomide in my
hand, the first thing that struck me, at the door of
the pharmacy on Avenue Junot, a few steps from my
doctor's house, was the sign on a little café on the
other side, 'Au Rêve'.

As I was walking, I saw once again T. in the days
before his death, in the room adjacent to mine, in
the small pavilion where we lived at the bottom of a
somewhat neglected garden. I saw him again, nestled
down in his bed, still, his skin ivory-yellow, curled up
and already strangely distant, and I saw him again a
little while later, at three in the morning, dead, his
limbs thin and skeletal, sticking out, spread-eagled,
abandoned, his belly enormous and bloated, his
head thrown back, his mouth open. Never had a
corpse seemed so non-existent, miserable remains
to be thrown like the body of a dead cat into a ditch.
Standing still in front of the bed, I looked at that head
that had become an object, a little box, measurable,
insignificant. At that moment, a fly came close to the
black hole of his mouth and slowly disappeared within.

I helped to dress T. the best I could, as if he were to
be introduced into high society, at a party perhaps, or
was about to go on a long journey. Lifting, lowering,
moving his head as I would have any kind of object,
I put on his tie. He was oddly attired, it all seemed
normal, natural, but his shirt was sewn up at the collar,
he had no belt, no braces, no shoes. We covered him
with a sheet and I went back to work till the morning.

Entering my room the following night, I noticed
that, by a strange coincidence, there was no light.
A., invisible in the bed, was asleep. The corpse was
still in the adjacent room. I found this lack of light
disquieting and, about to walk naked in the dark
corridor leading to the bathroom, which meant I had
to pass before the dead man's room, I was seized by
a terrible fright and, while not believing in it, I had
the vague feeling that T. was everywhere, everywhere
except in the pathetic corpse on the bed, that corpse
that had appeared so non-existent to me; T. had
no more limits and, in the frightening expectation
of feeling an icy hand touch my arm, I walked the
corridor with a huge effort, came back to lie down
and, eyes open, I talked with A. till daybreak.

In another way, I had just experienced what I had
felt a few months earlier in front of living beings. At
that time I began seeing the heads in an emptiness,
in the space surrounding them. When for the first
time I clearly noticed the head I was looking at
freeze, permanently still, I trembled in fear as never
before in my life and a cold sweat ran down my back.

It was no longer a living head but an object I was looking at as any odd object, but no, differently, not like at any other object, but as something alive and dead simultaneously. I screamed in anguish as if I'd just crossed a threshold, as if I had entered a world never seen before. All the living were dead, and this vision repeated itself often, in the underground, in the street, in a restaurant, in the company of my friends. That waiter from Brasserie Lipp who froze, leaning over me, his mouth open, with no connection to the previous moment, or the following moment, his mouth open, his eyes staring in complete stillness. But at the same time as humans, the objects underwent a transformation: tables, chairs, suits, the street, as well as trees and landscapes.

This morning when I woke up, I saw my towel for the first time, that weightless towel in a stillness never noticed before, and which seemed to be suspended in a frightening silence. It no longer had any connection to the bottomless chair, nor to the table whose feet no longer rested on the floor, barely touching it, there was no longer any connection between the objects now separated by immeasurable chasms of emptiness. I looked at my bedroom with terror, and a cold sweat ran down my back.

A few days after having written in one go what you've just read, I wanted to go back over that story and rework it. I was sitting in a café on the Boulevard Barbès-Rochechouart where prostitutes have strange legs, long, slim and slender.

A feeling of apathy and hostility prevented me from rereading my text and reluctantly I started describing the dream differently. I tried to say in a more precise and striking manner what had touched me; for example the volume, the thickness of the brown spider, the density of its hair that appeared pleasant to the touch, the position and exact shape of the stretched web, the expected and feared appearance of the yellow spider, and most importantly the shape of its scales, a shape of flat and rippling waves, the odd combination of the head and the acuity of the right leg as it moved forward. But I wanted to say all that in a way that was only emotional, to make certain points memorable, but without looking for the connection between them.

Discouraged, I stopped after a few lines.

Some black soldiers passed by in the fog, that fog which the previous day had filled me with a weird pleasure.

There was contradiction between the emotional way to depict what made me hallucinate and the sequence of facts I wanted to narrate. I found myself facing a chaotic mass of time, events, places and sensations.

I tried to find a possible solution.

First I tried to name each fact with two words that I put in a vertical column on the page, but that didn't lead to anything. I tried to draw little boxes vertically too, that I would have filled gradually, striving to

situate all the facts simultaneously on the page.
There was a problem with the time element and I
endeavoured to situate it all chronologically. But I
always struggled with the tube shape of the narrative
that was bothersome to me. Time in my whole story
went backwards, from the present to the past, but with
returns and ramifications. In the first story, for example,
I hadn't found a way to introduce the Saturday lunch
with R.M. before my visit to the doctor.

I had told my dream to R.M., but on reaching the
moment when I buried the remains, I saw myself
in another meadow, surrounded by thickets at the
edge of a forest. Pushing the snow aside with my
feet, digging the hardened ground, I buried a barely
nibbled piece of bread (the bread stolen in my
childhood) and I saw myself running through Venice,
holding tight in my hand a bit of bread I wanted to
get rid of. I walked across the whole of Venice looking
for the remote and solitary neighbourhoods, and in
one of them, after several missed attempts on the
little-known small bridges, on the edge of the darkest
canals, shaking from nerves I threw the bread into the
stinking water of the last branch of the canal enclosed
by dark walls, and I ran away, in panic and barely
conscious. That brought me to describe the state I was
in at that moment. Telling the story of the journey
to the Tyrol, the death of Van M., see note (that long
rainy day when alone, sitting before a bed in a hotel
room, a book by Maupassant on Flaubert in my hand),
I looked at Van M.'s head transforming (the nose
more and more accentuated, the cheeks hollowing, the

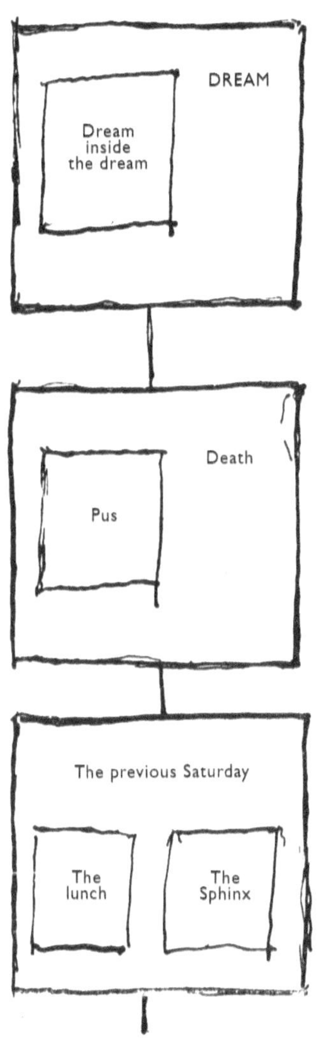

DREAM
Dream
inside
the dream
Death
Pus
The previous Saturday
The
lunch
The
Sphinx

open mouth almost still barely breathing and, towards evening, trying to draw that profile, I was suddenly very scared at the thought that he might die), the stay in Rome the previous summer (the newspaper I happened to see by chance and which had a news item stating they were looking for me), the train to Pompeii, the temple of Paestum.

But also the dimensions of the temple, the dimensions of the man who suddenly appears between the columns. (The man appearing between the columns becomes a giant, but the temple is not reduced in size, the geometric scale no longer applies, and this is the opposite of what happens in St. Peter's, in Rome, for example. That church's empty interior seems small (this is particularly visible in a photograph), but men become ants and St. Peter's does not become bigger, only the metric dimension counts.)

This led to a discussion about the dimension of heads, the dimension of objects, the relations and differences between objects and humans, and with that, I ended up on what I was particularly concerned about, at the precise moment I was relating that story at that Saturday midday.

Sitting in the café on the Boulevard Barbès-Rochechouart, I was thinking of all that and was trying to find a way to express it. Suddenly I had the feeling that all the events existed simultaneously around me. Time became horizontal and circular, and it was space at the same time, and I tried to draw it.

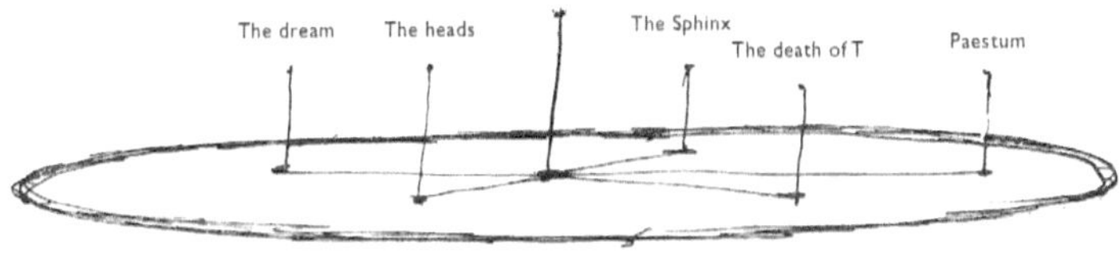

The café on the Boulevard
Barbès-Rochechouart
The dream
The heads
The Sphinx
The death of T
Paestum

I left the café shortly afterwards.

That horizontal disc filled me with pleasure and, as
I was walking along, I almost saw it simultaneously
under two different aspects. I saw it drawn vertically
on a page.

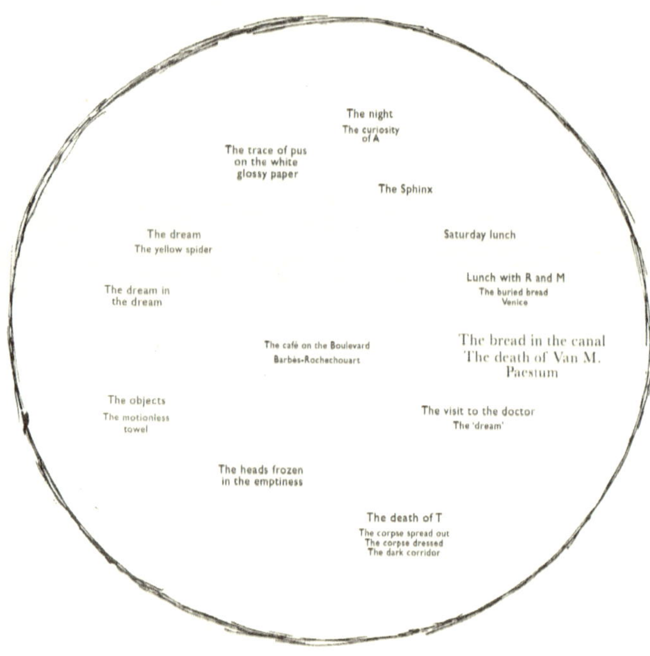

But the horizontality was what I was after, I didn't
want to lose it and I saw the disc become an object.
A disc of two metres in radius, give or take, divided
into segments by lines. On each segment was traced
the name, date and location of the event to which it
corresponded, and on the edge of the circle, in front
of each segment, a panel was erected. Those panels of
various sizes were separated by empty spaces.

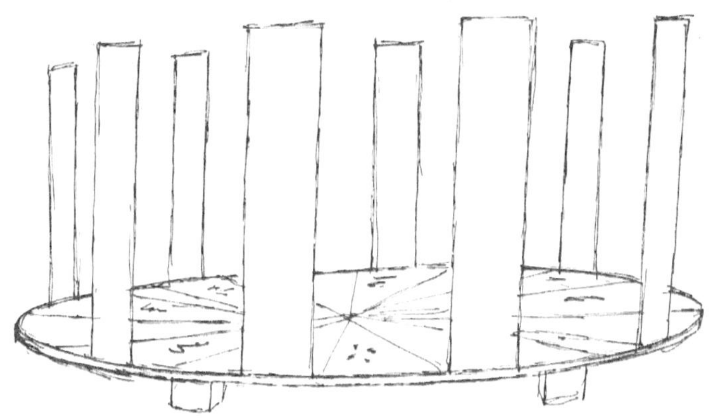

On the panels the story corresponding to the segments was developed. With a rare delight I saw myself walking on that space-time disc, reading the story presented before me. The freedom to start wherever I wanted, for example, from the dream of October 1946, and then to go the whole circumference, and end up a few months earlier in front of the objects, in front of my towel. The positioning of each fact on the disc was very important to me.

But the panels are still empty; I don't know about the value of the words, nor their reciprocal relation in order to be able to fill them in.

Note: This journey I made in 1921 (The death of Van M. and all the events surrounding it) has been like a gap in my life. After that everything turned to something else, and that journey became an obsession that lasted a whole year. I never tired of relating it and often I felt like writing it, but that remained impossible. Only today, through dreams, through the bread in the canal, has it become possible for me to mention it for the first time.

First published in *Labyrinthe*, no. 22-23, December 1946

ANDRÉ MALRAUX

ALBERT SKIRA GENÈVE

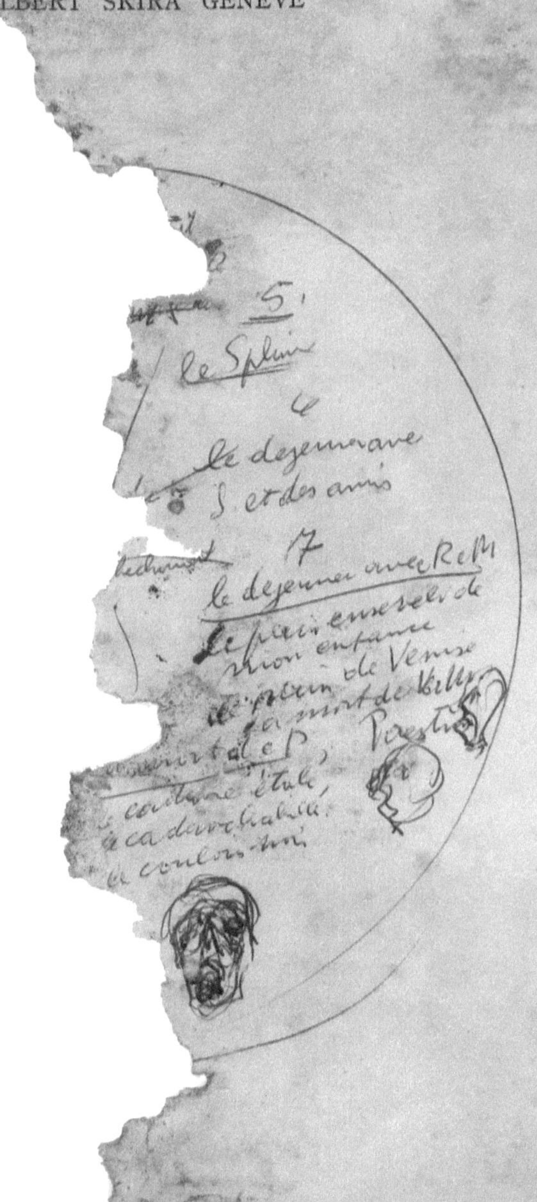

Enquiry on the encounter

Could you tell me what has been the main encounter in your life? Up to what point did and does that encounter give you the impression of fortuitousness? Of necessity?

A white piece of string in a pool of cold liquid tar haunts me, but simultaneously I see, walking past, one October night in 1930, the gait and the profile – a little bit of the profile, the concave line between the forehead and the nose – of the woman, who since that moment has unwound, like an uninterrupted line, through each space of the rooms that I was. That encounter gave me and still gives me, in spite of the surprise and the astonishment, the impression of necessity. It seems to me that each encounter that has touched me has presented itself on the day and at the precise moment of its necessity.

Minotaure, no. 3-4, 12 December 1933
(Question by André Breton and Paul Eluard, answer by Alberto Giacometti)

<u>Coal of grass</u>

In the middle of the day I turn round in the void and look at the space and the stars that run through the liquid silver surrounding me, and Bianca's head that stares slightly behind in the echo of her voice and the feather steps near the red wall in ruins.

I go back to the constructions that amuse me and live in their surreality; a beautiful palace; the parquet of white dice with black and red dots on which one walks, the rocket-like columns, the ceiling in the clouds that laughs and the pretty, precise mechanics that serve no use. Feeling my way I try to catch in the void the invisible white thread of the marvellous that vibrates, and from which escape the facts and the dreams with the sound of a brook on small, precious and living pebbles. It gives life to life and the shiny play of the needles and the revolving dice are formed and follow one another alternatively, and the drop of blood on the milky skin, but a piercing cry rises suddenly that makes the air vibrate and the white earth tremble. The whole life in the marvellous ball that envelops us and shines at the corner next to the water-jet.

I'm looking for women with a light step, and a polished face, who sing, mute, their heads slightly tilted, the same who existed in the little boy who, with his brand new clothes, walked through a meadow in a space when time forgot the clock; he stopped at a point and looked inside and outside at so many marvels. Oh! Palace palace!

Le Surréalisme au service de la révolution, no. 5, 15 May 1933, p. 15

The brown curtain

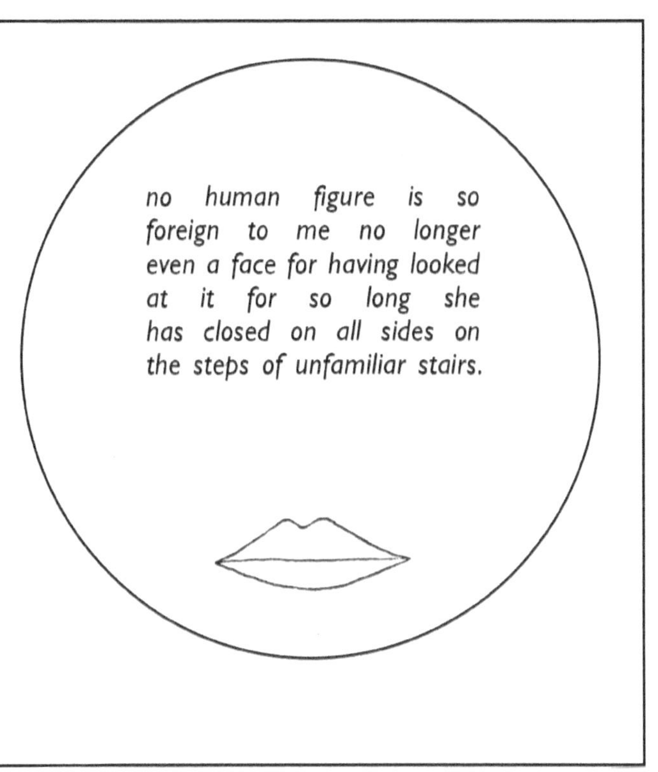

no human figure is so
foreign to me no longer
even a face for having looked
at it for so long she
has closed on all sides on
the steps of unfamiliar stairs.

Poems in 7 spaces

Poems in 7 spaces

2 claws
of gold

a drop
of blood

white spiral
of gust on
two brestasts
crying out

the yellow
meadow
of
madness

3 black horses gallop

the feet of
the chairs break
with a
dry cracking

all the objects have gone far away
and a woman's footfall
and the echo of her laugh leaves
the ear

Yesterday, quicksands

As a child – between 4 and 7 years old – I saw the
external world only through the things that could
contribute to my happiness, especially rocks and trees,
and rarely more than one thing at a time. I remember
that, for two summers at least, I could only see among
the things surrounding me a big rock that stood 800
metres or so from the village; that rock and the objects
directly related to it.

It was a monolith of a golden colour, opening onto a
cave at its base: the whole lower part was hollow, the
water had done its work. The entrance was low and
elongated, barely as high as us at the time. At certain
spots the inside space was even more hollowed till
it seemed to form a second little cave at the very
back. It was my father who showed us the monolith
one day. It was a huge discovery. Straightaway I
considered that rock as a friend, a being motivated
by the best intentions towards us; calling us, smiling
at us like someone we used to know and loved dearly
and with which we were reunited in boundless and
joyful surprise. Immediately we became exclusively
preoccupied with it. From that day, we spent all our
mornings and all our afternoons there. We were five or
six children, always the same, and we were never apart.
Every morning, as I woke up, I looked for the rock.
From my house I could see it in all its detail, as well
as, like a thread, the little path leading to it; everything
else was vague and inconsistent, air that attaches
itself to nothing. We followed the path without
ever deviating from it, and we never left the ground

that immediately surrounded the cave. Our prime
preoccupation, after discovering the rock, was to
establish the entrance. It had to be a big enough gap
to let us enter, but not bigger. And I was bursting
with joy when I was able to squat in the little cave
at the back. I was barely able to fit in; all my desires
were met. Once, I don't remember the reason why,
I wandered further from the cave than usual. Shortly
after, I found myself on a height. In front of me, a
little further down, in the middle of some bushes,
there was a huge black stone shaped like a narrow and
pointed pyramid, whose faces fell almost vertically.
I cannot express the feeling of chagrin and defeat I felt
at that precise moment.

The rock immediately struck me as a living, hostile
and threatening being. It was threatening everything:
our games, our cave and us. Its existence was
unbearable and I felt straightaway–not being able
to make it disappear–that I had to ignore it, forget
about it and mention it to no one. However, I moved
close to it, but it was with the feeling of indulging
myself in something reprehensible, secret and seedy.
I barely touched it with one hand, with repulsion and
fright. I circled it, trembling at the idea of finding
an opening. No trace of a cave, which made the rock
even more intolerable, but I felt a kind of satisfaction:
an opening in that rock would have complicated
everything and I could already feel the dejection of
our cave if we cared about another one at the same
time. I ran away from that dark rock, I didn't mention

it to the other children, I shut it out and didn't go
back to see it.

*
**

At the end of that same period, I was impatiently
waiting for the snow to fall. I was restless until the
day I judged it was enough – and I misjudged it a few
times before – to go alone, carrying a bag and armed
with a pointed stick, to a meadow located some
distance from the village (it was all about a secret job).
There, I tried to dig a hole just big enough for me to
enter. On the surface, only a round opening, as small
as possible, would be visible, and nothing else. I was
planning to lay down my bag in the bottom of that
hole, and once there, I imagined that place to be
very warm and dark; I thought I would experience
a great joy… I often felt in advance the illusion of
that happiness on the previous days; I spent my
time figuring out all the techniques needed for that
construction, I was mentally doing all the work down
to its smallest detail; each gesture was experienced
beforehand, I imagined the moment when I would
have to take precautions to avoid the whole lot
collapsing. I was so happy seeing my hole completely
arranged and ready to enter. I would have liked to
spend the whole winter there, alone, confined, and
I thought with regret that soon I would have to go
back home to eat and sleep. I have to say that in
spite of all my efforts, and also probably because the

external conditions were adequate, my desire never
materialised.

At the beginning of my schooling, the first country
that seemed wonderful to me was Siberia. There
I could see myself in the middle of an endless plain
covered in grey snow: there was never any sun and
it was always very cold. The plain was bounded on
one side, quite far away from me, by a pine forest, a
dull and dark forest. I was looking at that plain and
that forest through the little window of an isba (that
name was very important to me) in which I was
standing, and where it was very warm. That was all.
But quite often I transported myself mentally to
that place.

As repeated mental temptations of the same order,
I remember that at that same time, for months
on end, I couldn't fall sleep at night without first
imagining having gone through a thick forest at
dusk, and reaching a grey castle standing in the
most hidden and neglected place. There I killed two
men unable to defend themselves, one was around
seventeen, always looking pale and scared, the other
wearing armour on the left side, on which something

like gold was shining. After having torn their dresses, I raped two women, one was thirty-two, all in black, her face like alabaster, then her daughter, on whom white veils floated. The whole forest resounded with their cries and moans. I killed them too, but very slowly (it was night time then), often next to a pond with green stagnating water, which was in front of the castle. Each time there were slight variations. Then I burned the castle and, satisfied, fell asleep.

Le Surréalisme au service de la révolution, no. 5, 15 May 1933, p. 44-45

Inferiority complex
regarding women,
always ~~to be~~
to have a woman
again and <u>life</u>

1933-1934

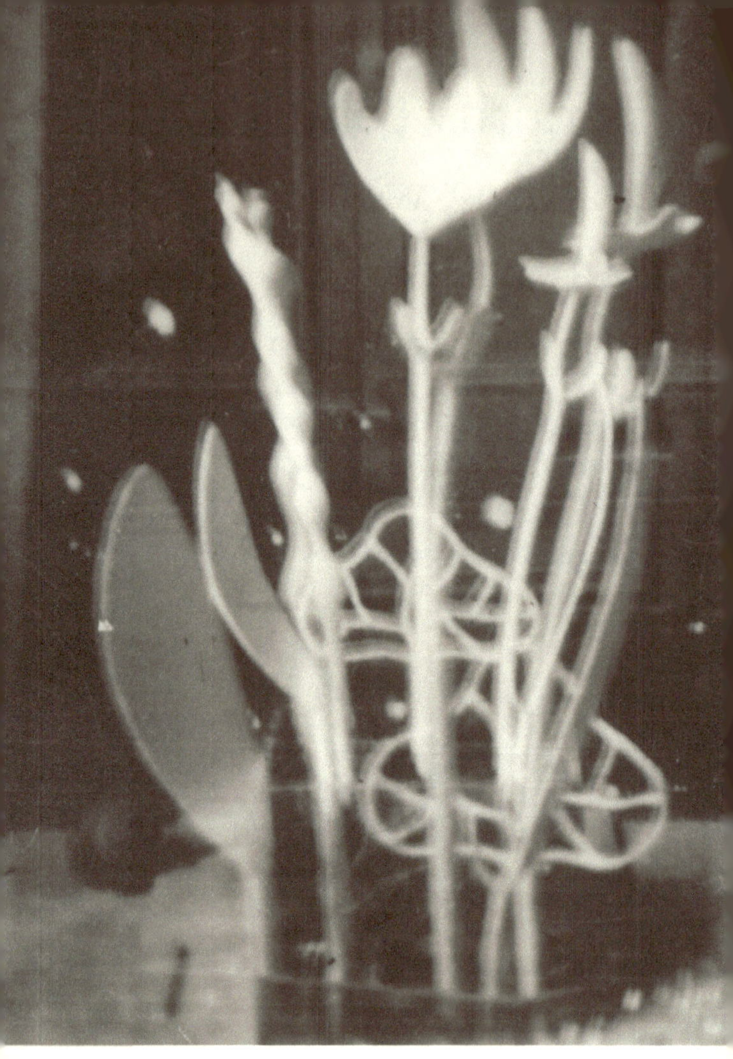

Plaster flowers, c. 1931–1932
Unknown photographer
Fondation Giacometti Archives

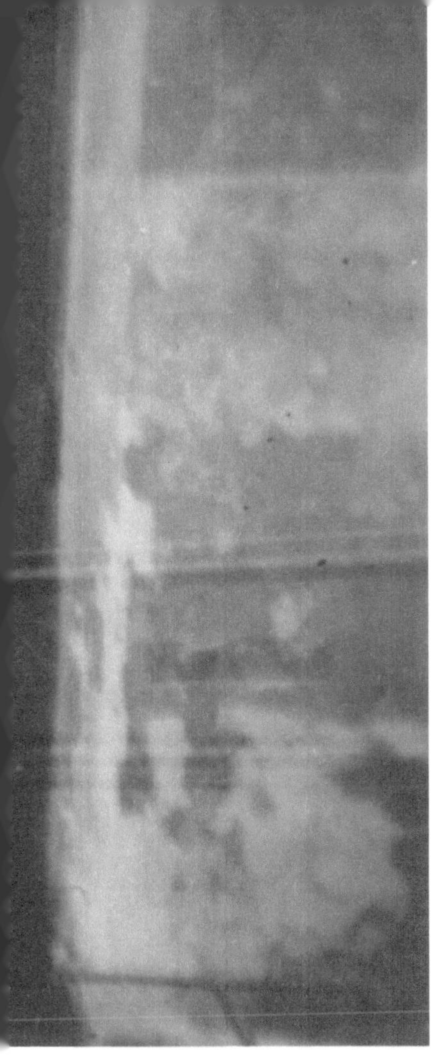

woman eats son
son licks woman
man penetrates woman
woman absorbs man
on the same level

Around 1932

<u>Outside all control…</u>

Outside all control… etc.

I think that sentence by Breton in I.M.S. *[first Manifesto of Surrealism]* remains today, and especially today, entirely relevant.

Our activity is nothing but a perpetual question to the universe that is also us. For each of us, the world is truly a sphinx in front of which we always stand, a sphinx that continually stands in front of us and which we question. We can only do that with the sustained, even physical attention of all our being, on the lookout, ~~like a faun~~, and with ~~total~~ availability as great as possible on all levels… And we record what we hear and even what we believe we hear.

We can also compare the world to a crystal block with countless facets. According to one's structure and one's position, each of us can see certain facets, certain parts of the facets and his painting poem object etc. is only the record of what he catches sight of. It's obvious that all the facets seen by a group of people at a certain time must be very close to one another, barely small differences of angles, inclinations, and seen from afar, they just form one single clear mass in relation to all the countless that are plunged into the darkness of space. The production of each of us is the exact reflection of that difference in angles and position.

What can stir our passion is to discover a new edge, a new space, the smallest part of a new space, to catch sight of it in the darkness as the light barely grazes it. It is the sphinx that, here and there in the distance, pronounces a word out of its enigma, and all those words constitute human knowledge. And that knowledge is a very tiny glimmer always flickering in the dense, heavy unknown that surrounds us, that touches us, that penetrates and envelops us and fills each of our atoms. The obsessive fear of getting to know the perpetual question is truly innate to us as for the plant, one of the thousand movements it does to exist. I would really have trouble conceiving the smallest difference between the activity of the plant and our activity. I do think that all human activity is just a mass of movements, mechanical, automatic reactions as blind or as little blind as the movement, as the reaction of a leaf, an atom of stone.

We are interested in certain things, and rather in those than in others because our constitution compels us, because it would be quite impossible for us to think, to act any different. Just like we don't have the choice over the length of our legs, our ailments, we don't choose our way of thinking, our way of expressing ourselves, and that obsession to express oneself is of the same nature, rigorously the same nature as the movement of the flies around the globe of the lamp turned off in the morning.

Around 1930

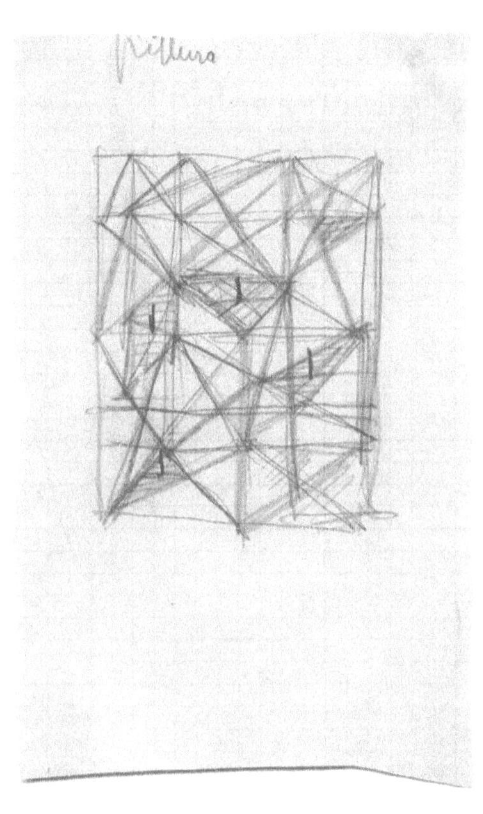

Geometric drawing, 1932-1933
Lead pencil on graph paper, 13.7 x 8.5 cm
Fondation Giacometti

Splinter of sphere of the golden apple in ~~the sun~~
the light
Feet of chair, wood that's smashed to bits
ripped off
Breathing, in the street (avenue du Maine)
in front of the cinema (the posters in all the most
violent colours) a dog
short, grey, dirty and curly-haired walks
slowly along the wall, on the other side
two eyes of light watch it, in a
brown coat a woman passing at the same
moment behind the iris of its eyes
but there remained the empty grey paving stone,
in the front window the sun
the wicker basket
the footsteps followed on the pavement that turns into
the next street, the other all open in front,
in the snow on a square the neck moves forward
new boots the doubt
at one metre fifty paving stones on the vertical
the horizontal, width between shoulders 80.
but the veiled laugh that quickly runs and disappears
in front of us on the horizon its echo resounds
~~a moment after~~ immediately after in the ear.

Around 1930

Fear, death undulant crystalline…

fear
death undulant crystalline
I think about women
she brings her head close to my ear
her leg, the big one
close distant there
plane of space and time backwards
they talk they move
here and there
but it's all gone.

going up to the bedroom
looking for the oil
the pastilles for the teeth
the suspensory bandage
for my balls
all that tonight still
before going back ~~to the studio~~
[erased part]
and my friends
(36.8, no temperature)
a little pain in the shoulder
comfy in bed.
pencil in mouth

(my legs)
she was stroking her neck
and shivering
but round as apples, as pears
touch the threads
they are white

very fine
careful!

dead grey empty cries full
rings pan pan tan grey empty
cries
cries empty grey rings dead
open

and then stretched
they sleep
or they die
also sometimes
one from time to time
pac he falls
in a void, rather
the space neither
in small dots.

And they walk along
quickly a little bit
all with eyes
and two legs perhaps
which carry them
on a line
elsewhere

through on a line
in the distance
that's all
and the ashes

of bones and cigarettes
(always somewhere
they move)

cannot be exhausted because of the bath
it must be somewhere?

In every dimension
Always
Not
With nothing

I shall get up
I shall go to the café
Perhaps I shall see Denise
(the bombs at the Louvre)

not to write it then
to shout it

[what follows is illegible]

Lulu, Lulu!...

Lulu, Lulu! Come down and close your suitcase…
it's Nénette!
it's Nénette?
          (music on a loudspeaker)
tim, tim…
Madeleine!
it's not hygienic heyheyhey!
Good morning sir
You're leaving?
You're not offering me anything?
So you're okay, Sir?
… That's what you say…
… There's no one.
are you okay?
Come with me I'll give you a hard-on hihihi!
ha-ha-ha-
A little bit
… me this morning
hahaha!
ah! no!
Nelly! Nelly! Nelly! !
Wait, wait wait
Let me go
it's me who brought…
huhuhu!
well!
… a hundred francs…
I've heard Madame… forbad…
(slaps, laughs)
… give me…
… my friend…
oh!!!

you've aged
         (dirty bald man)
I'm waiting
we pull ourselves out
Cloakroom! Cloakroom!
no no no
I in any case
oh but I
ssst
Yes (blond woman whistles to the music.)
But it's okay! It's okay!
Listen to me!
Listen to me!
… because you…
hey <u>sit</u>!
leave it, it's for the sweeper
no no, he's not here
There there
here he comes
oh!!! I say
Lallala!!!
         (whistles)
ah! ah!
         Pierrot!
Nelly listen, what's he called, that one…
laughs
bet you, bitch!
after me I am a…
a what?
I am a pus (?)
all broken my rubber's all broken
That's nice

hahaha!!
the boyfriend's waiting for someone
Ah! the bastards!
That's a nice waltz, that is
I said, that's a nice waltz
that a nice waltz
I shall punch you in the face!…
I say
      (woman whistling)
Ginette! Ginette! Ginette!
tilialala…
la la lallala (whistles)
Miss!
Miss!
Violette! Violette!
Ginette!
that's all they like heyheyhey!!
no surely!
Well!
I'm off to clean up
Oh well
Telephone! Telephone!
Oh yes! yes!
Die können überhaupt nicht danzen, da hinten
[Anyway they can't dance, at the back]
… leave soon…
    ~~early~~
certainly not!
     oh no
I say no! hohohoh!!!
    Damn
Good morning gentlemen

…well look at my hair…
ha la la
no, no no oh
a match?
The pigs, that's the only thing they like
so
makes me feel hot
There's Mister Paul here…
oh yes…
Let's not exaggerate, right
It's all very well
It's rare…
that's true
Hey look!
…they failed
Marion!
oh! ah!
          heyheyheyhey!
Nénette!
Nénette!
hohoho!
üh!!!
Ginette sst!
Since there was no one.
ohho! ohoh!
hey Marion!
ohoh!
Marion hey!
oh hüü!
<u>the door!!!</u>
oh I beg you!
it's the door that……

at what time
…the most loyal
…20 minutes…
well
ah I have no money left I can't. I have no money left
<u>(a woman speaking)</u>
Ginette!
Spit it out!
oh ohhohoho!
ah the sigh!
well, well
in Buffalo at the back motorbike
I'm telling you
well the type of football
there what's he called
oh
bring me Sonia…

Fragile fragile canopy of glass…

fragile fragile canopy of glass cloudy
Violet unsure discreet gait
point where everything's at stake – with endless caresses
sex glass cloudy delicate of glass sex
the gait with the gait of swamps
that disappear in the sleeps of hotels
imponderable sleeps
they are black the shreds that are floating
softly in a sleep breath of morphine
delicate breath panting with morphine and the sheets
I see I see the hotels the sheets
uncertain paths of sex, flowers
nay nay
pale flowers of flesh under the stones.

The Invisible Object, c. 1934
Unknown photographer
Fondation Giacometti Archives

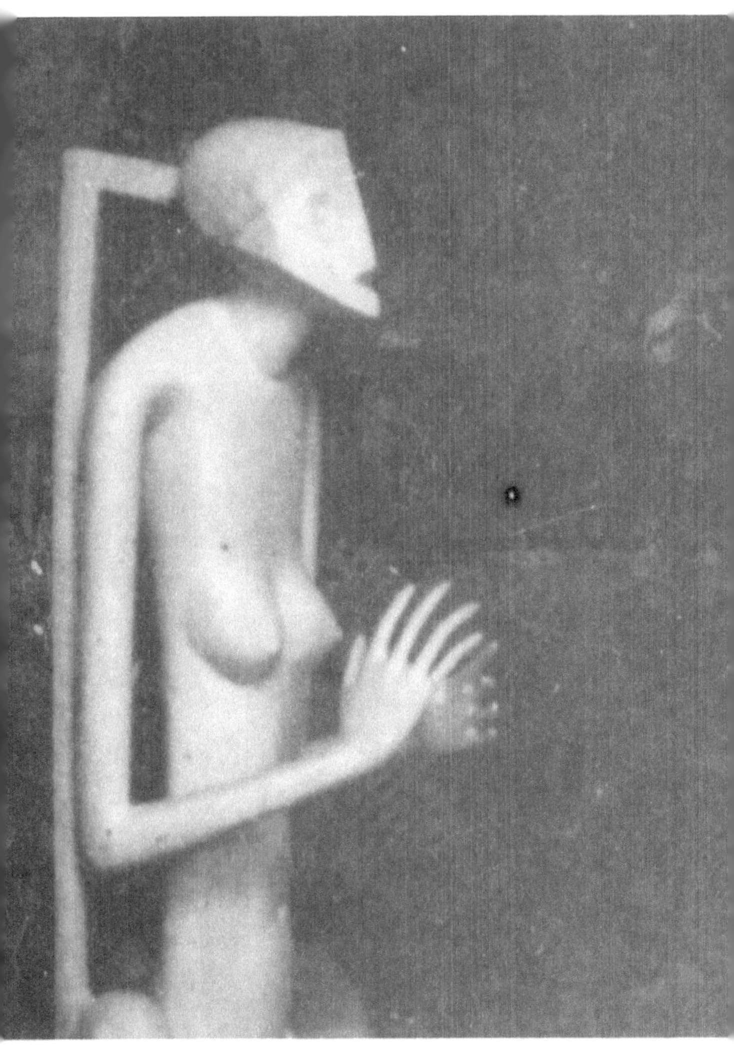

I'll write new things,
they'll take shape against
religion, homeland and
capitalism that's obvious,
against politics that's
obvious, but I want
something else, new
revelations, I shall have
them and then I shall
exhibit new sculptures
soon all new ones

1933-1934

Translated from French by Paul Buck and Catherine Petit.

ISBN : 979 1 0370 1683 6

www.ingramcontent.com/pod-product-compliance
Lightning Source LLC
Chambersburg PA
CBHW030401160726
47992CB00007B/2912